Visions Unseen

Aspects of the Natural Realm

Frances Ripley

FINDHORN
Press

First published in English by Findhorn Press in 2007.

ISBN 978-1-84409-093-8

A CIP record for this book is available from the British Library.

Edited by Jean Semrau.
Cover design by Damian Keenan.
Interior design by Frances Ripley & Thierry Bogliolo.

Printed and bound in Scotland.

Published by

Findhorn Press

305a The Park
Forres IV36 3TE
Scotland, UK
tel +44 (0)1309 690582
fax +44 (0)1309 690036
email info@findhornpress.com

www.findhornpress.com

1 2 3 4 5 6 7 8 9 10 11 12 13 14 13 12 11 10 09 08 07

Seed I

Dedicated to the Earth,
and all Beings who dwell therein.

Matumba

Acknowledgements

In a publication of this kind it is difficult to fully acknowledge the enormous debt of gratitude owed to so many, who, both knowingly and unknowingly, gave of themselves so generously and lent such continuous courage and conviction to my creative work. In addition to those named and remembered with such affection and respect in this book I must first acknowledge my mother, Olive Ross-Smith, whose caring attention and introduction to the richly abundant flora and fauna of my childhood Scotland gave me the necessary initial faith in my own appreciation and insight into the wonders of the natural world.

Others I must thank include Albert Harloff, Colin Louis, Edmund Harold, Mara Pearson, and Rachael and Ruurd Bekemer. In the development of the book itself I would like to acknowledge the early encouragement and editing advice of Amanda Gamley; and May East for her extensive efforts to find a publisher for a Portuguese language edition. Also, Colin Brown of MMS Graphics, Elgin, for his unlimited patience with my perfectionism! More latterly, and most of all, I must acknowledge Sheila Phelvin and Richard Penny for their hugely intelligent and delightfully good humoured skills, working from the chaos of my raw materials! Thanks to Imogen Masters for her editing ability. Last, but by no means least, I would like to thank my husband, George, for his long-suffering patience and quiet support as this work slowly took shape within the loving shelter of our wonderful home at Findhorn.

Table of Drawings

Table of Contents

Preface

It was with great joy that I accepted Frances Ripley's invitation to write this Preface to her beautiful book, with its highly evocative title, *Visions Unseen*, so provoking of our curiosity. My first motive for responding positively to the invitation was that the book constitutes a great contribution in defence of Nature. In second place comes Frances' affirmation of her inspiration by the unseen Beings who taught her that the Nature Spirits and Devas are of such infinite variety that they are impossible to measure. The third reason for my acceptance was that Frances found a truly original way to make "the unseen" seen, in transforming her intuition of these Beings into the beautiful pictures reproduced in this book. In the language of transpersonal psychology I would say that Frances worked on a different level of consciousness, in which it was possible to transform intuition of the unseen presence of Beings into the dimension of common reality. In other words, she has made visible for us the invisible world by which she has been inspired. Finally, I believe that Frances has made an original contribution to the Artistic field, especially if we take into consideration that her production is quite different from the so-called "automatic drawing" techniques frequently used in artistic-spiritualist productions. I warmly commend this book to all who share the re-awakening interest in communication between the visible and invisible worlds that surround us.

—Pierre Weil, Unipaz-University for Peace, Brasilia

Foreword

I was honoured and delighted to be asked to provide the foreword to this book. It documents Frances Ripley's experiences and insights into a world rarely discovered by casual observation. Although people living in rural cultures have never completely lost touch with the presence around them of intelligent beings integral to the landscape and to its flora and fauna, most of us are challenged by the idea of nature spirits or "the world of faery". It is directly contradicted by the scientific materialism which permeates our culture and which tells us that we are wrong to believe in anything that cannot be quantified, probed and measured in a laboratory.

So when mystics and seers report encounters with invisible beings, can they be taken seriously? How can we discriminate between pathological hallucinations, and those impressions which truly convey information from hidden depths of reality?

Esoteric tradition does indeed speak of vibrational rates which enable different states of matter to interpenetrate. This is not utterly different from the multidimensional theories of superstring theory which suggest that whole universes interpenetrate and coexist alongside each other in inconceivably small spaces.

Frances tells us that in certain states of consciousness she becomes aware of various beings who are part of the life of the natural world and who enable her to create images of themselves; thus making themselves visible to her and also to us. Her story of how this artistic gift developed is fascinating. For me it is especially so since we have parallel gifts, and it is wonderful to see how different yet similar our experiences are.

Her gift developed spontaneously, well before she heard about Findhorn and its founding principle of working in conscious cooperation with the intelligences of nature. A few months before she first came to Findhorn in 1973, I left the community to enter a nearby Benedictine monastery, ostensibly to escape the by then worrying level of perception into this world that had developed for me. So her drawings did not in any way imitate or reflect any influence from the ones I had done during 1971: a set of symbolic drawings inspired by the Devas.

Clearly, both she and I were directly prompted by the ever more urgent pressure of these Intelligences of Nature to provide images which, along with statements from Dorothy Maclean's meditations and the tales of experiences of Pan and the elementals from R. Ogilvie Crombie (aka ROC), might make them more accessible to Findhorn residents and visitors.

I did not meet Frances until some time in the 1980s when I also saw her drawings for the first time. Recognition was instantaneous. Her images came from the same reality that had reached out to me in 1971. Despite using quite different techniques, our images have a clear family likeness.

We also discovered that we both had been endorsed personally by Ogilvie, who said to each of us that we had drawn what he saw. To all who knew him personally, Ogilvie's warm friendship is a remembered joy. His endorsement continues to be a shared honour and privilege.

More than thirty years on, the true significance of this kind of breakthrough is much clearer. Frances is one more witness to a reality which urgently requires our attention. The damage suffered by the environment has become close to irreversible as far as human effort is concerned. The only real hope for healing it lies in embracing a new reality which encourages and welcomes experiences of nature consciousness, whether of Gaia, as representing the totality of life on the planet and all the systems and forces which sustain it, or of individualised godlike nature beings, through whom we can imagine and with whom we can co-create solutions to climate breakdown.

I hope the images Frances was inspired to provide will make this easier to imagine.

May her story be an inspiration to all who read it.

—Brian Nobbs

Introduction

This book features reproductions from original drawings that are inspirationally given by Nature. Over the years, my many encounters with the Unseen Beings have taught me that the Nature Spirits and Devas are of infinite variety. Some could startle us with their strangeness and some are of inexpressible beauty. The range of Beings of the Nature Kingdoms is endless, from tiny Elfin Beings that live inside flowers, to Devic Beings so vast we could not measure them.

They also have the capacity to show themselves in a variety of forms, or else as formless swirls of colour and light, and this helps to determine the quality and intensity of the drawing. Other determining factors are how they choose to manifest themselves and where they choose to be, and also the degree of receptivity and understanding of those to whom they are revealed.

We are shown that these superjacent Beings reveal themselves by coming to be drawn so they can be known as realities profoundly related to our own. As people who look upon these prints become aware, we can share the joy of the Devas and other Nature Spirits – and grow to seek their co-operation both in tending gardens and in restoring the balance of nature on the Earth.

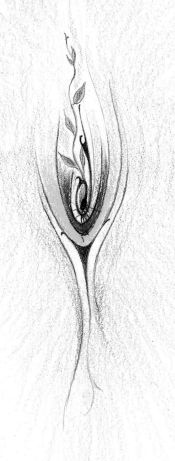

Seed II

Prologue

Sitting in my house on Findhorn Bay surrounded by the pine trees, it is November and a crisp, clear day. Almost all the deciduous leaves have fallen and we have just hung out the first birdseed and peanuts for the approaching Winter. This morning seven kinds of bird have already returned to our garden to investigate and sample what is on offer.

As I watch, with a great sense of immediacy, I am aware of re-awakening interest in past events – events that have helped to shape our emerging perceptions at the dawn of the twenty-first century. I am talking about the "thinning of the veil" between the visible and unseen worlds – and the small part I was given to play.

Over the period from 1966 to 1992 during which I was drawing the ethereal beings, I experienced a wide range of psychic, emotional and physical sensations. It is not easy to express in words these subtle and sometimes elusive phenomena, so what follows can be little more than an attempt, an approximation, at describing what was going on.

It is important to understand, too, that people who illustrate the Spirit World work in many differing ways, which demonstrate the diversity and complexity of relationships between other realms and those of our own. My particular process leads me to stress that I never in any sense *depicted* the Devas and other ethereal beings that appeared to me. I did not see forms outside of myself from which I made marks on the page, thereby creating a likeness. For me, what was essential was to be sensitive to, and identify with, a particular feeling emanating from the Being to be drawn.

Dramatic changes in my pulse rate would signal when I was to sit down and draw. It could become either slower or faster, on occasions almost doubling in speed. My mind would enter a state that was, paradoxically, both clear and focused, open and sharply aware. This is a tenuous and delicate state of consciousness, a positive receptivity – the very essence of meditation.

In this state I might experience a ball of light, a clear lens of vibrancy and vitality. Of necessity one finds here a compromise between the physical and metaphysical worlds. That which is ethereal and intangible is endeavouring to be expressed through the limitations of a material substance – the *pigment*.

My hands would become very restless and my fingers begin literally to itch! In this highly integrated and sensitised state, I would run my hand over my box of crayons. Nearly always starting with a black pencil, my hand was then directed to the colours I was to use. One in particular would stand out from the others. The drawings *manifested* themselves and were completed in one sitting. There was no reworking or improving of the image on the page. There exists an innate perfection in what had been spontaneously expressed through me at that moment in time.

I have been asked if I used a *Spirograph* to draw the sweeping lines. The answer is that at no time in any of the drawings did I use any instrument, neither did I use an eraser. I did not turn the paper while working, so the drawing always remained in either its original horizontal or vertical position. The sweeping lines were all drawn freehand.

With hindsight, I now comprehend the process a little better. What seemed to happen, was that the Beings I was to draw were obliged, as it were, to reach in from another dimension to be with me, and I would adjust to reach out to meet their dimension. Ethereal Beings are in the fourth dimension, as I understand it. We are in the third. In "radio" terms I was tuned into a higher frequency.

In the case of Devic Beings – responsible for the archetypal imprints of the animal, vegetable and mineral creation – the frequency is even higher. Therefore, contact with these Beings can have an intense effect upon the nervous system. R. Ogilvie Crombie told me to be careful not to allow contact to take place too often, and to space the opportunities I gave to these superjacent Beings, as they have no understanding of time.

Over the years, I learned that when I was in touch in this way – whatever took place, and from whatever level – it was important to have at least the same amount of time to myself, quietly alone, to readjust back to myself, and to be "earthed" before moving back into more mundane worldly experience. To act otherwise was a severe shock to my nervous system, which at times ended in severe migraine. It took me some time to realise that this was the cause. I discovered that placing my hands in cold water or on the earth could aid my re-adjustment to our normal frequency.

One could liken the process to the way in which a rainbow appears in the sky, or how Lewis Carroll describes the benignly surreal appearances of the Cheshire Cat, in *Alice through the Looking Glass*. It has been speculated that this phenomenon came from Lewis Carroll's migraine headaches. But whether these phenomena come from the headaches, or the headaches came from the phenomena, I believe I was blessed with an "overlighting" Presence, or "guardian", that regulated and protected me. Or was it that I became stronger and more aware of how I was inspired to serve the Unseen Worlds?

I still seem to require absolute peace and solitude to make contact, and need that even when recording my experiences. As I write this, thanks to the loving support of family and friends, I am fortunate to have the essential solitude of a tranquil house. The recalling and sharing of my experience is the reason for this book.

Star of Michael

Starting Out

I come from Scotland – from Edinburgh to be exact. My father was originally from the Highlands – Dingwall, just north of the Black Isle, near Inverness – and my mother was English, from Bedford. During the Second World War I was sent to a school in Dunkeld, that occupied a large house in extensive grounds by the River Tay.

Wildlife abounded. Slipping off – not so easy with school discipline – whenever I could along woodland paths to see rabbits and squirrels, and to revel in the azaleas and rhododendrons set under huge trees, was a joy.

In the winter the deer would come right down round the house. Strangely, I never remember anyone else even mentioning the beauty of this abundance and the golden opportunity it offered to study nature. We were too busy on intellectual matters. However, it gave me the foundation, and for that I am grateful.

Upon leaving school I returned to Edinburgh and started training in Physiotherapy. The War was still on and this would be of service in the War Effort, as the wounded servicemen were returning. My three brothers had all been called up in 1939 at the start of the War, so the family at home was incomplete and there was much anxiety for their safety. After a year of the training I reluctantly had to accept that Physiotherapy was too demanding, emotionally and physically. I could have been conscripted into the Women's Services or the Land Army but was pronounced unfit, which did nothing for my self-confidence! However, I picked myself up and realised I could now attend Edinburgh College of Art, and was accepted there to take a three year course in Design and Crafts. I greatly enjoyed my major subject, copper wheel glass engraving, and a range of other subjects. During this time we made frequent trips to the Royal Botanic Garden, where I made a great many drawings of the plant life, exotic flowers and lovely trees to be found there. Choosing a quiet spot alone I could happily lose myself in the work.

Leaving college I began to feel the split in my life, seeming to be on the edge of all that was going on, and finding it hard to keep up with the crowd. Always happier on my own, I was told I should mix and join in. I could not keep on with the Glass Engraving, finding the crystal now too expensive and largely unavailable with most of it going for export. Having to earn my living, my artistic career appeared to be at an end.

After a series of soul-destroying jobs of various sorts, I started teaching handcrafts to homebound disabled people for the Edinburgh Red Cross.

This taught me a lot about relating to people from all walks of life, and living in all kinds of places. It was heartbreaking in one way, but very rewarding as well.

During this time I joined a group working mainly on spiritual healing and occasional "Rescue Work". Rescue Work may be regarded as necessary in cases of sudden death where, no longer on Earth, those in transition have no understanding of their new dimension. It was a unique group with a wonderful teaching that I was able to bring into my work at the Red Cross. I was also told that I would draw again but in a very different way. I suppose I didn't really want to know. I buried the idea and for years forgot this was even mentioned

Then an offer came to go up to London, to the Headquarters of the Red Cross Welfare Department, working as Officer for Handcrafts and Holidays for the Disabled. The answer to my prayer, I snapped it up. Needing to move away from home and really be responsible for myself was to prove a lot tougher than could ever have been imagined. But the South was the right place to be, and whatever happened I was going to stay there and work it through – learning a great deal along the way.

My first home was a single room, in a shared house with four nurses in Kent. Forbidding, perhaps, in my Red Cross uniform, I never managed to get more than "hello" from any of them in six months! The South was a big shock to my Scottish being. Simply unable to start a conversation in a train or in a café, I felt myself and others to be shut away. Enduring the rush hour trains, standing closely packed with strangers, clattering full tilt up to London had to be experienced to be believed. Seeing home only at night and working most weekends, how to survive?

Desperately needing to move closer to the metropolis and really wanting to live in Kensington, I yearned to be near the London parks. The offer of a room, sharing a flat in Chelsea with two ladies, sounded wonderful. So off I went. The

Chelsea flat, however, proved a nightmare. On the ground floor, with buildings being demolished all around us, the rats rushed in and out from under the floors. With a seemingly endless number streaming through the house, strangely enough they never once came into my bedroom. But it was time to move again.

During this difficult time, however, a life-changing event happened. I discovered the Spiritualist Association, situated just around the corner from my office – offering a library, lectures, meetings, café and book shop. And, above all, a friendly welcome! Many people in London had their clubs at that time. Making the Spiritualist Association my club opened up all kinds of opportunities, and nourished what I felt was my real being.

My need to move house had again become pressing and at the club I met a friend with whom I had been at Edinburgh Art College. Living in a Kensington house divided into single apartments, she knew of someone who was about to return to South Africa. She would ask the landlady. A fortnight later I moved into the biggest and best room in the Kensington house. I couldn't believe my luck.

This was to be my London home for the next eight years. We were almost a family with a landlady who was very good to us all. But respectful of each other's "front door" we could easily have peace and quiet when we needed it. This was luxury, with all the advantages of the Kensington – and Holland Park just up the road! I still had to travel by underground in the usual squashed up manner but it was only five minutes to Hyde Park Corner where I worked. Like most Londoners I went to the Parks as much as I could, and always greatly appreciated any invitation to spend weekends out in the country.

Able now to make more of my life, one side of me was very busy. It was the Centenary Year of the Red Cross Society – 1963 – and there was much to do, but it was very interesting to be a part of it all, with gatherings of many nationalities with fascinatingly different views of life. The other side of me was drawn to spiritual matters, developing new contacts with people who were to become loyal friends and give me wonderful support and encouragement. My new friends made it possible to tolerate, and then to enjoy my London life. I had found my niche.

How it Began

The year 1966 was to prove a turning point. Harrods in Knightsbridge was within easy walking distance of the office. Warm, and full of quality goods of all kinds too dear for me to buy on my small salary, there was no charge for feasting my eyes on the beautiful things! I could at least afford the freshly baked wholemeal bread, still warm from their bakery – my only indulgence.

On one of my frequent trips to the store, I stumbled upon the Art Department. I had been feeling more and more in need of colour in my life, and I became fascinated with the huge range of paints, crayons and pastels on sale. The widest selection of colours was in a box of pastels. Although it was expensive, on impulse I bought a small box. But my box of pastels proved a disappointment; I just could not get anything like a picture. Whatever did I buy them for? I gave them away.

All became clear a few days later when my wanderings once more led me into the Art Department. Again I was like a child in a toyshop, this time pouncing on a huge box of *water-colour* crayons with thirty-eight, or more beautiful colours of the spectrum. I had buy it! *This* was to become the medium I had been seeking, and have worked with ever since. That evening I went home clutching my special box not quite knowing why I had bought it, but feeling convinced that this time my intuition had spoken to me.

After dinner I sat down with some trepidation to see what I could do. After all, I hadn't drawn anything pictorial for twenty years. At that point I realised I had been so excited by my purchase, and so disconnected from practicalities, that I had forgotten to get any suitable paper. So I simply made do with notepaper, deciding I would just let my hand do its own thing.

Or was it me who decided?

I scribbled away on a number of sheets and felt really good doing it! The following evening, having bought some proper drawing paper
I scribbled again. And so it went on for several days, as I gradually focused in on the page. Then patterns began to form, groups of swirling lines in all sorts of colours and interweaving shapes.

Soon I was shown in a very clear way that I was not just scribbling for fun. I drew a very distinctive pattern, balanced with a *magenta* drop in the centre. Without knowing the recipient at all, but feeling it was right, sometime later I was moved to give this drawing to a member of my Spiritualist group. Upon seeing it he asked how I knew about the *magenta* shape. Telling him that it had just "come" like that, he told me it was exactly what he saw as he went into his meditations. Evidently there was something happening here. He had verified spontaneously that my drawing was of an internal image, personal and significant to him alone.

During this time I was handling many letters in my work from the sick and disabled. I thought I would try holding one letter at a time and see what might happen. Sure enough, I received patterns quite different and distinctive for each letter, with accompanying information, mainly about the sender's emotional state of mind. Touching into the emotional field – *fear, frustration, envy, jealousy, anger* and *guilt* – it seemed to me that these might be the causes of disease in very many cases. Even with a so-called "accident", the original cause seemed to be emotional.

Working in co-operation with a healer for a few months, to help him with his clients, I paid attention to what I was picking up. Being highly sensitive, very soon I found myself overloaded with other people's difficulties. It was often alarmingly difficult to distinguish between my own problems and theirs. Advised to let this way of working go, I had clearly seen how deep wounds of the emotions might become deep wounds of the body. Healers can certainly help in these cases, but ultimately the true healing is our own responsibility. We have to heal ourselves.

Throughout 1967 I continued attending meetings and lectures at the Spiritualist Association, and mixing with my new found friends. One evening to my surprise the Association secretary asked me if I would be prepared to sit on the platform and introduce Mr. Ronald Beesley, a respected healer and lecturer.

I did not know Mr. Beesley personally, but the Association appeared desperate to find a stand-in, so it had to be me! I went to the lecture room door to take the tickets and receive our distinguished guest. Unusually, Mr. Beesley arrived early, giving us time for conversation. Attuning to his surroundings, he looked enquiringly at me. "What is your particular interest?" he asked.

"I like drawing, and love to be out in nature."

"You should come and stay with us."

I jumped at the invitation. "Yes, I would love to!"

After introducing Mr. Beesley to the Association audience, I heard a very special lecture, ending with an equally powerful guided meditation that took us to the very bridge between Earthly and Cosmic understanding. To be seated beside him was a great privilege. The evening heralded a new phase in my life, something different, touching into another Realm. As with the box of crayons, I didn't know to where or to what I was being invited, but I knew quite clearly that I was going to go there as soon as I could!

Making enquiries, I found Mr. Beesley's place to be a kind of healing retreat near Tunbridge Wells in Kent, where guests could stay for a week. It was there, to *White Lodge*, that he had invited me. Taking leave from my work I went down the following weekend.

The house was hidden away in a wooded country area, peaceful and beautiful. There were eight guests of all ages. The first thing we discovered was that there were no planned activities except meditations morning and evening held in the Sanctuary, which we were welcome to attend – after all, we were "having a rest". We were not even allowed to help clear the tables and wash up. To the workaholics amongst us this was quite a shock, almost an insult! What had we come to? Worse still, we were asked to be in bed by nine. Affection and respect for our host won the day, however, and we decided we would give it a try.

Although one or two people were edgy and disagreeable at first, by the third day we were all enjoying our new-found freedom, doing only what we felt like doing. And we found we were all sleepy by 9:00pm.

It was a magical transformation, and by the end of the week we had become a very close group. This very lovely atmosphere felt so close to *nature*, and one afternoon I discretely vanished into the garden with my crayons. I wanted to be out of sight and undisturbed. Seated by the pond, for a time I watched the wildlife – birds, spiders, frogs and dragonflies of many colours. I felt content and welcome. Birds came close, and there seemed to be an interest in my being in that particular place in some way. I could feel a *presence* around me, friendly, lively, inquisitive. Then, feeling to draw, my mind was at once absorbed but clear. Focused only on the paper, in pencil I started to draw in an unconventional way.

> *The drawing grew into a bright little face,*
> *With pointed ears and a big smile.*

Continuing to follow my impulses, I moved onto the crayons, working in with the colours intuitively and into more detail. All colours of the spectrum were used, but the predominant colour was *blue*. The picture developed to include a kind of hat. More part of the Being's head, and unlike hats as we know them, the headpiece would have been quite impossible to "remove". While drawing I felt so joyful and light. A big, blue dragonfly landed close by and seemed to be watching me, staying for quite a while, undisturbed by my movements.

With the drawing complete, I just sat and basked in the wonderful feeling of bliss and peace. I seemed to have a heightened awareness of all that surrounded me. Realising that the time for Meditation approached I packed away my things, and slipped into the house and up to my room. No one was to know of my drawing! Laying the work on a table, to really look at what had happened, I felt the greatest astonishment. I may have been to Art College, but even I knew that *I simply couldn't draw faces!* Did I really draw this bright, lively Being? I couldn't believe it!

As we were enjoying our after-dinner conversation in the lounge, a member of staff entered. Excited, she at once approached me and asked:

"Where did you get that drawing?"

"What drawing?"

"The one on the table in your room."

I asked why she was interested.

"Because it is *Lennie*."

"Who's *Lennie*?"

"Don't you know? He is an Elf that lives in the garden. He often sits close to the house."

"Actually, I drew him this afternoon," I replied with some embarrassment. My questioner had blown my secret to the entire group!

At the same time it dawned on me that somehow I had drawn a Nature Spirit that I had not actually seen, but which had been clearly recognised by someone else, and which was known to members of the Community. Whether or not I believed in Fairies, this was something much more definite. "Believing" is usually what you have been taught in stories, but *Lennie* was known, named and accepted by all those who lived in the house. And somehow I had just drawn him.

> *I call the Nature Spirit "him",*
> *Because the word "it" is too impersonal.*
> *I believe nature spirits are androgynous, they just are.*

I was overwhelmed. Part of me wanted to hug myself and the other part wanted to run away! Of course, everyone promptly asked if they could see the drawing, and did I have any more?

> *Some believed me,*
> *While others thought*
> *I was telling fairy stories!*

As far as I was concerned I was still half in the realm of the Unseen, and my sensitivity was beginning to falter. As I bumped back to Earth again that night I started to cry and cry, and I am not sure any of us understood what was happening, least of all myself.

I loved *Lennie*. He was a delight, but he does not appear among my collected drawings – I gave him to Mr. Beesley. He also recognised *Lennie* as soon as he saw the drawing. It needed the two verifications to convince me!

❋❋❋

Very reluctantly I travelled back up to London, and my other life. No one at home would have believed my experience, and certainly I could not mention it at work. *Yes, I had had a very nice restful week's holiday, thank you.* Head down and get on with earning my living.

But the office did not feel at all like *living*. Had it all been a dream? But I had the receipt for my railway ticket. It had really happened!

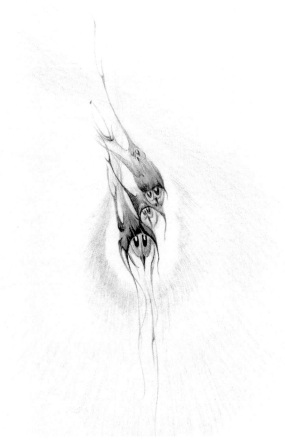

Insect Kingdom

Connecting with Unseen Worlds

Having struggled with my *double life*, now, interestingly, my Red Cross work started to ease off. Moving into a different office at the top of the building gave me my own room, and more time alone. Evenings and weekends I would draw or study spiritual matters, go to my club, and – when he was in London – attend Ronald Beesley's lectures.

Living still in the middle of London I kept working during the day, but now gave all of my spare time to my connection with nature. Far more than just the Nature Spirits, somehow I was now tapping into the *whole realm* of Nature. All kinds of drawings started emerging in the same way, with me never knowing what was coming next.

During this period, working on deep *blue* paper, the colours were filtering onto the page as manifestations of Spectrum light. They glowed with purity and clarity. With Earth pigment as the only available medium, however, by their very nature the true expression of the essential qualities of these Spectrum light manifestations always eluded me. The manifestations included the *Crown of Progression* (see p. 93), the *Star of Hope* (p. 63), the *Star of Peace* (p. 91), the *Star of Michael* (p. 17), and the *Cup of Remembrance* (p. 33), among others.

Others came which were like rockets shooting off into the Cosmos. They came throughout 1968. These rocket drawings (see p. 44) seemed to be speeding me up. My heart would beat faster, and it was as if I was being lifted up away from Earth into *outer* space.

After completing the second of these I found I was to take a large sheet of *white* paper.

> *I began to draw a face,*
> *Intense, beautiful and magnificent.*

Impossible to express in mere words, this Being was drawn in pencil – a striking face with intense eyes. The face was set unusually low on the paper. Colour was given and a form of head-dress added, tall, like a blade, encasing the entire head right down over the shoulders. All the colours of the spectrum were there, but predominantly blue and pink. The drawing was full of light, not substance, translucent and luminous. I had to stay completely focused on the paper, intently drawing for three-and-a-half-hours, while this Being's wonderful presence pervaded my being.

Asking his identity, the reply was, "I am an *Emissary from Jupiter*".

✳✳✳

Staying with me for quite a time I was overwhelmed by what was happening, but greatly welcoming the privilege and thanking the *Emissary* for his visit as best I could. It was a full day before I was restored to my normal self, although the joy remained with me for some while after. Was I mad? Yet, the *"Emissary from Jupiter"* had come in the same way as the other drawings. My pulse rate was markedly increased, and I got frightened in my aloneness.

> *This is crazy, I cannot go on like this.*
> *Please, please, let me go!*
> *Leave me alone!*

I pleaded with all my heart, and, *bang!*, that was just what happened.
A void. Being left alone for some weeks was a relief, to begin with.
I could get on with my "normal" life, domestic chores, writing letters, going out and visiting friends, and so forth. And, most importantly, doing my job effectively. But I soon began to realise that I had done a dreadful thing – broken my connection with my drawings. Depressed, sad and miserable, I felt very guilty.

> *What had I done? I didn't want this life.*
> *I belonged in the spiritual life,*
> *working with the drawings and nature!*

Would I ever be able to restore the connection after being so rude and ungrateful? I hit an all-time low, and my back was really bothering me. I was totally out of balance and deeply depressed.

Emissary of Jupiter

Then, discovering that Dorothy Smith was back in this country, I managed to arrange a sitting with her. A medium with whom I had previously closely bonded, Dorothy was highly thought of. Working partly in London and partly in America, she was regularly invited to speak at the annual Remembrance Day Service at the Royal Albert Hall. When we met, Dorothy immediately asked me what on earth had happened. She began by saying one thing: *"You cannot break your connection with the kingdom of nature, it is a part of you."*

So there was hope! I had – *above all* – to forgive myself. Then, lift myself up, apologise, and invite the Beings to come close again. Putting out my crayons, I allowed things to evolve. The next evening, still feeling rather dead, I took a pencil and started scribbling – *doodling* – as one does on the telephone book. This went on, and gradually I realised that little faces of all kinds were appearing on the paper – a swirling flow that I knew to be the *Collective Nature Energies*.

It was wonderful to feel again the Kingdom of Nature, showing me that its inhabitants were responding, wanting me to know they were still there, and all waiting to welcome me "Home". My feelings of heaviness began to lift. To my understanding, my awareness of the connection had been restored. I had simply not understood that the Realms of Nature do not perceive time, as we know it. Nor, indeed, what we call "working hours"!

And so I had to make a clear decision. How much time was I to give to tuning in and drawing? How much could my being comfortably sustain? Being too much available caused imbalance, and damage to my nervous system. Being too little available brought depression, and ultimately despair. I decided to devote my weekends exclusively to spiritual work for the Kingdoms of Nature. Being very clear with myself about this, from then on I was undisturbed during the week. With my work at the Red Cross less intense, and with fewer times away from home, I was again able to accept invitations from friends and attend lectures and meetings with groups of like mind.

Dorothy Smith suggested she give a lecture at the Spiritualist Association with slides of my drawings, to make my work more widely known. We went ahead. I made the slides, and we had a date for the lecture. Dorothy was very fully

Collective Nature Energies

occupied when in London, and somehow we never managed to get time together to discuss the drawings and their meanings in detail. The day duly arrived, and, meeting in the Association café for the afternoon before the lecture, we were still jotting down notes on the back of a napkin! We were barely halfway through when we were interrupted once again by someone else urgently needing Dorothy's attention. As she was rushed away, she called over her shoulder, "Don't worry, it'll all be all right. I'll say just what comes to me – see you tonight."

Needless to say, we both forgot the napkin!

Getting to the lecture theatre early, and anxious to set up the screen and projector, I found the room already filled to capacity. An exciting and unnerving experience, but a lesson in trust!

With Dorothy at the front waiting to speak, and me at the back working the projector, I had no idea of the import this lecture was to have on my life. As the slides came up, Dorothy described in great detail all that I had received, and a good deal more. She was gently showing me how little I was conscious of what I had been in contact with – Cosmic Realms of beauty, light, and deeply meaningful Symbology. Glancing up I distinctly saw Dorothy shining in a pink aura, enveloping and reaching out all around her.

> *Feeling raised up and expanding with her,*
> *I felt overwhelmed by an indescribable sense of complete connection.*

Approaching at the end of the evening and introducing himself as Dudley Jevons, a gentleman asked if he could see the originals of the drawings we had shown. We made an appointment. I did not then realise the great importance this meeting was to bear on my future life.

When Mr. Jevons arrived, he asked to be left quietly on his own, to really study and tune in to each picture. Afterwards he told me that he felt he had taught me to draw in a previous incarnation. Appointing himself *guardian* of my gift, and subsequently often checking up on my work, Dudley wanted me to meet his son David, and new daughter-in-law Anne. Anne and David turned out to have been members of a group formed by Dorothy Smith in New York, where they had recently married.

Cup of Remembrance

The Farm

Coming to live in Hampshire, England, Anne and David planned to start a Meditation and Study Group. They were looking for like-minded people to meet and work together to refurbish their house and small farm.

I was delighted to be invited to stay for a weekend, and a group of us spent hours doing up the conservatory and greatly enjoying each other's company. I went over about once a month, each time it seemed as if Anne had added at least one more animal to their menagerie! Besides two horses, there were a friendly goat, a cow, chickens, and a large black Great Dane, all of which I enjoyed. We had wonderful meditations and transmissions, but we were there mostly to work. We refurbished the barn and sheds and prepared the vegetable garden in exchange for spiritual teaching of an advanced order.

My spiritual side nourished, I began to do more drawings. One evening I drew the *Woodland Elf*. This Being illustrates how nature spirits can look very different, and sometimes quite strange, to us humans.

❋❋❋

Back in London, leaving work one Friday evening, I began to feel very strange, not quite fully present and in a state of tension all over. Was I coming down with some virus? Completing my shopping I quickly went home, deciding to take the weekend quietly.

After a small breakfast on Saturday morning I still didn't feel too well. In an attempt to relax, I listened to music, and time somehow vanished. No lunch, a cup of tea, and so on till evening. Then, with the familiar sign of my heart speeding up, I fidgeted around, pacing apprehensively. Deciding to eat properly, I made a good-sized scrambled egg on toast. Just as I was about to dig my fork in, a voice in my ear clearly stipulated, "Crayons".

So that was it. I was not to eat but to draw.

Obediently I took out my drawing materials and began.

Woodland Elf

What emerged on the paper
Was a striking face with blue-green eyes…

…so intense that I felt I couldn't take their penetrating look. Covering all but the face was a luminous and slightly transparent head-dress. containing all the colours of the spectrum. It was like trying to draw the quality of a rainbow. I was so overwhelmingly and calmly absorbed that I forgot to ask who this being was.

Some three hours later I began to "come back" to where I was. Re-heating my interrupted meal at one-thirty on Sunday morning, I asked myself:

What was this, what was happening to me?

I went thankfully to bed. Later that night

I awoke with a loud, clear and beautiful note,
Reverberating through all my being.

It sounded like a huge tube being hit with a soft hammer. On and on it sounded. This happened at least three mornings in a row, gradually becoming fainter and fainter.

I found myself compelled to take the picture to Dorothy Smith. I wrapped it carefully and took it straight to the Spiritualist Association, where I found Dorothy standing at the door. I said, "I have something to give you."

Taking the envelope, she replied, "Not *'give'* to me – what was actually said to you?"

"Well, it was to *'take'*…"

"Yes," she said, " *'take'* doesn't mean give! Now let us see what it is."

Going in at once to open the package, Dorothy exclaimed, "I know who this is, it is a *Master of Sound!*" Then, "This *Sound Being* came to me in New York just before Anne and David's wedding, and he chanted through me, in trance, 'The Song of Creation', a wonderful, powerful song."

a master of sound.

f. Ripley 1968

A Master of Sound

We compared notes on what it felt like to be approached by such a powerful being, and found that our experiences had been nearly identical. Dorothy described feeling like a lion within a cage, unable to stretch to contain the energy.

✳✳✳

It was deeply reassuring to share these experiences, and again receive complete confirmation that I *really* was being contacted to draw the unseen beings. Once more I felt overwhelmed.

> *Why me?*
> *And what are they coming into my being for?*

I knew the drawings were not just for me, that I was only the instrument and custodian of them.

My frequent visits to the Farm in Hampshire inevitably drew me closer to the nature kingdom and particularly to the animal kingdom. At this time I was not a vegetarian but I did enjoy vegetarian meals. I used to go to the shops on Friday to buy enough food for the week, store it and work my way through the selection. One Friday I got home with my trolley-full only to find I had forgotten to get any meat or fish. *Well, why worry? I had beans and cheese and lots of vegetables and fruit.* The following week the same thing happened. I did not fully register it, but somehow I went over to eating all vegetarian food without consciously doing it.

On the way to the station to catch my train to work I had to pass three butchers' shops. It was a very busy road, but I took to crossing over and walking on the other side till I got to the station, and only then crossing back again. I had never liked going into butchers' shops but now I couldn't bear being near them. I would feel sick and find tears in my eyes. I had to rush past, it was as if I could feel the animals' anguish.

About seven weeks into my new vegetarian diet, and with my pulse rate slowing, I could feel that perhaps I was going to draw again. On the Saturday, late evening, I sat down with my crayons. The drawing started with what looked like an Afro hairstyle, which went on for some time, possibly till I released speculating what it was going to be! Then it continued with a beard and moustache. Tantalisingly it went on building up and eventually the marvellous eyes were included and finally the star on the forehead. I was feeling an amazing sensation of gentle strength and compassion.

As I understood this beautiful Being, it was the *King of Beasts (see next page)* – no doubt called various different names. Not Pan, but one of his subjects.

I have seen this Being on a few occasions since, always related to animals. Not long after receiving the drawing I had a phone call from Anne in Hampshire, to say that their goat had a broken leg. She did not tell me which leg was injured, but they were waiting for the vet. Almost immediately, I saw the being from my drawing, the *King of Beasts*. I welcomed him and after a pause clearly saw the goat's badly broken back leg. Then a snake appeared and carefully wrapped itself round and up the leg, straightening and supporting it as you would with a plaster cast. In that moment I knew the leg would heal perfectly. To protect the leg the vet did put on a plaster, and it healed quickly and perfectly.

A clear case of co-operation between the two Worlds.

My powerful contact with the Unseen Worlds was now quickly developing. Writing a letter alone at my London office late one afternoon, I suddenly felt a sharp pain in the chest – it was like having my ribs broken, or perhaps a bad heart attack. Having calmed myself I realised it was not my own physical state – someone was in need of help. About to be locked into the building, I asked the Angel or *Spirit-Messenger* to please withdraw and let me be myself to travel home. I promised I would then help in any way. Feeling better, I then checked the time. It was just six o'clock.

Reaching home I rang my sister-in-law to enquire about my brother – though I could not explain why to her. My brother was in hospital and there had been complications, including a clot on the lung. *Yes, he was doing well and soon to be home.* Tuning in again I drew the same *Spirit-Messenger*, and asked that help be given in whatever way needed.

Letting the matter rest, the next morning I walked into my office and a few minutes later my senior officer called with shaking voice to tell me that a fellow member of staff, Pat, had been killed in a car crash the previous evening. She had been alone, and had died instantly. Asking the time of the accident I was told, "At six o'clock last night." Having met Pat's husband not long before *he* had died the previous year

I immediately focused on requesting him to come and "meet" with Pat, if he had not already done so. Feeling them both in that moment, and then a release, I was myself again.

✳✳✳

Having told no one of my experiences, I went to the *Spiritualist Association* that evening and attended the *Clairvoyance* meeting. I was not known in any way to the medium, but again I was asked at short notice to introduce her and chair the Meeting. Although the evening was keeping the medium very busy, I noticed her look round at me on one or two occasions. Finally she said, "I know I am not supposed to give a communication to my chairperson but this man is pleading so insistently I hope you will allow me. *Has someone you know been killed in a car crash very recently – yesterday – to do with your work?*" I said that this was true. She continued, "*Well, this gentleman is her husband and he wants to thank you for bringing him in touch with her to help and take her over.*" I related what had happened for the understanding of the audience, at the end of which the medium said, "*He says to ask you if you still have his tiny paintbox?*" After her husband's death, Pat had given me his watercolour paintbox, which I still use. Pat and I were the only people who knew of her gift to me!

✳✳✳

Although I had been out of touch for many weeks, at the Farm we had gathered a diverse group of very dedicated people from many walks of life. Even overlapping for only a few hours would enable us all to be together for our meditations.

King of Beasts

All through this time I had been feeling a close link with the Planets, and all that was going on. There was a lot of Space activity during this time, 1968–1969, and this was when I received the *Star* and *Rocket* drawings to which I previously referred. Feeling as if I was being taken away from Earth, way out into Space, my pulse rate increased considerably and I felt light and elated. The drawings, which I call *Rockets*, and which came to me on several occasions, usually preceded a drawing of a Planetary Being.

✳✳✳

At about 11:30 one evening, I began another drawing in pencil. As the wonderful face built up, a feeling of joy and light filled me as I drew – such strength, compassion and love. The head-dress was like a rainbow in that it was luminous and shining, and the point of the head-dress went right down the forehead to the Third Eye position.

Drawing intently for some three hours, and although again of course not seeing the being as I drew, I feel a closeness to him still, and sense his presence as I write. He told me his name was *Santos of Jupiter*. As mentioned earlier, the *Emissary of Jupiter* had of course preceded him.

Never ceasing to be staggered that such a being would choose to come through me to be recorded on Earth, as always I liked to seek proof of what had happened. The following day I telephoned Anne and, without giving any hint of connection or research, I simply asked, "Anne, who is *Santos*?"

"*Santos*", she said, "I know that name. David, who is *Santos*?"

He replied, "He's from the planet Jupiter. We have a transmission from him."

There were other drawings of Planetary Beings, but none so clear and arresting as the one of *Santos*.

Santos of Jupiter

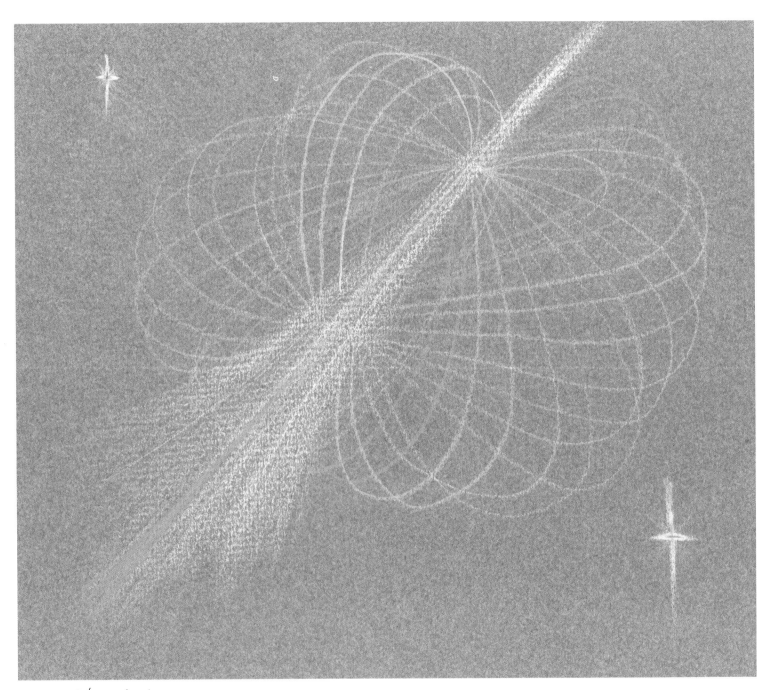

One of the 'rocket'drawings

Loss of the Nature Kingdom

Having worked in the Red Cross for fifteen years, and feeling drained and weary from six of those years in an office job, in 1969 I came to the conclusion that I really wanted a change in my life. I took a week's leave in June to mull things over. It was lovely weather and I spent time in the park every day, telling myself I would decide by the end of the week.

Having always wanted to work with flowers or plants, I made a few enquiries. No jobs were available without some training. So I rang the London School of Floristry. Yes, they had a short training course of two months, and a vacancy starting mid-July.

Leaving my position with the Red Cross required a month's notice. It fitted exactly. I decided to try floristry for a year, by which time I hoped to have a clearer idea what I wanted to do with my life. Upon leaving, several of the Red Cross staff with whom I had worked all those years said, "You are so right, I wish I had done the same thing when I felt like a change."

There was no doubt in my mind that the move from the Red Cross was correct. I needed to work with creations of Nature, hence my decision. I left happy, and started my new life. There were eight beginners and we got on very well. The School was just a mile across the Park and it was mid-summer. After our start at the School we were taken to a lovely flower shop in the centre of town. The smell of perfume and pot-pourri permeated everything. Completing our training in this heady atmosphere we received the widest experience of every aspect of the trade, even down to filling the bottles of perfume. At the end of our training two of us were offered casual work in the School's own floristry shop. As their top students, we took the offer for an honour!

Our new employment involved clearing windows and heaving large, two-to-three gallon buckets of flowers off shelves, many above our heads, and each evening taking some twenty of them through to the back of the shop for the night. Any romantic ideas we had had about floristry went out of the window with the buckets!

Having had enough of being treated like a slave after six months, I re-visited another shop I knew in town. Their standard of work was one of the highest in London, and I liked the owners. *Yes, they would like to have me and I would be given an extra training in their style.* The new shop had a very different feel. One of the owners had a big garden and brought in huge boxes of unusual garden flowers, branches and shrubs, fresh picked and quite different from market flower supplies. By including a proportion of these lovely treasures in amongst the commercially grown flowers, an *arrangement* became transformed and individual. I really enjoyed the training. The work I was given was mainly wedding bouquets and all sizes of arrangements. I was then placed in the kiosk of a big London hotel, which was vastly different to my first position.

About six months later, although I moved out of London to a smaller shop in Surrey, the work had become arduous and over-demanding. My love for flowers was very real, and is so to this day. But I did no *drawings* whatsoever in this period, and *a year to the day* from embarking on floristry, I gave in my notice to quit.

> *I saw now that Nature Spirits were no longer present*
> *in the cut, dying forms of commercially-produced blooms.*

I only remembered afterwards that one year had been my original intention. *The timing had been unwittingly precise!*

The Mineral Kingdom

Although I felt greatly relieved to have freed myself from the florists' world, the challenge remained…

How to be true to Nature,
and make my living?

My mind went to possible contacts who might help me to find another job quickly. I rang a friend in-the-know in the handcraft teaching field, to see if she had any suggestions. A wise lady, she suggested that later on there could be a vacancy in a Day Centre that she knew quite a lot about in Brighton.

When I asked if I could go down and see the Centre, she arranged a visit straight away. I arrived to find the Centre in a great state of anxiety. They told me that the person who had been teaching handcrafts had just died in a sudden accident. *"You see we're rather desperate to fill her place, because our disabled people can't be just left unattended. If you're interested, how soon could you start?"*

Within the week I found myself in Brighton, once more teaching Handcrafts, living in a small but wonderfully sunny flat on the fourth floor of one of those bow-fronted Regency houses right on the Kemptown seafront. With a view overlooking nothing but ocean, I was certainly *close to the Elements!*

Although the work was challenging, I enjoyed being back amongst a good cross-section of people. It was demanding and rewarding work, helping many people who were severe casualties of war to realise they still had the ability to produce creative work. We had a lot of fun together.

With my little flat only minutes' walk away I was also overjoyed that I could now afford to have a telephone of my own, and even a small car. Able to keep in touch with friends and the spiritual groups in Kent, Hampshire and London, I began to feel a lot more human. *And, in my peaceful little flat, I began to draw again.*

At this time I had a sharp lesson in the power of Minerals. Wandering one day round the intriguing shops in what is known as the Brighton "Lanes" I came across an *Aladdin's cave*, full to the brim with gemstones both cut and uncut. I was inside before you could say *abracadabra!*

When I asked about Cairngorms, a handful was spread on the counter for me to look at.

"Feeling" my way through them I said, to myself mostly, "No, I don't like the feel of that one, this one is better."

The lady behind the counter looked quizzically at me, but with a lovely smile, and asked, "So you 'feel' stones? That's interesting. May I ask what you do with them?"

Up to then not actually having done *anything* with stones, I mentioned that I did a little drawing. The conversation was fascinating. June, as she was called, knew a great deal about stones, including the effects of holding or wearing them.

As fortune would have it, June was about to give a lecture in some private venue and wanted to have slides for her talk. She was not able to take the necessary pictures herself, nor did she wish to pay for them to be done professionally. As I was itching to feel into all of the stones, we struck a friendly bargain. I would provide the skill and equipment for the photographs, and June would let me handle as many stones as I liked.

After closing time we took all of the photographs, casually observed by a couple of police officers watching through the window. Perhaps they had nothing better to do, but I imagined them watching my hands – after all, June really knew nothing about me.

Exploring more of this *Aladdin's cave*, I could feel the strong vibrations, and the concentration gave me a bit of a headache. June got all her pictures and was delighted. Her lecture was enriched and very well received, and *I was given the loan of six stones to take home*. Not knowing what would follow, I set up my crayons and paper. As I draw with my *left* hand I took a stone in my right hand. For each stone I got a small, but very distinctively different, pattern of lines in various colours. I could feel a very particular vibration in myself with each one.

Next day, in returning the stones to the shop I took along the drawings as well. Saying nothing I laid the drawings out in a row on the counter. Intrigued and

Cairngorm

very pleased, June pointed to one drawing and said, "That must be Topaz. The shell pattern is quite definite, and the rays of the sun too." I had no idea what she was referring to, but realised that in fact I had clearly drawn a shell and also sun rays. She then told me that in order to test if a Topaz is genuine you place it in liquid and it will vibrate the surface in the form of a shell and rays.

Here for me was further clear confirmation
That I was not just imagining what I drew.

I was also told later that if someone needed gemstone energy for healing, it would be possible to gather the *vibration* from the drawing. No need to have the actual stone, though presumably the presence of the stone would be stronger.

One day a large crate had arrived straight from Brazil. June told me it contained chunks of newly mined Amethyst. As she had not had time to open the crate, I offered to help unpack and discovered a treasure-trove. There were thirteen massive rocks of still-wet Amethyst. Removing the sawdust, I dried them all and polished them up. That was a lot of contact with all these big rocks., and there was no doubt I could feel the effect. A little like too much caffeine!

I had greatly enjoyed this unique and exciting opportunity but had to leave immediately afterwards to spend the weekend with my Hampshire friends, David and Anne. Although feeling stretched I managed to drive there all right, but when I arrived Anne said, "I don't know where you have been but you certainly have brought an unusual feeling with you!" About half an hour later I was completely knocked out with the worst migraine I had ever had. They had to steer me to bed. I was terribly sick and dizzy for about three days. I finally managed to drive home somehow, and ever after I have had a considerable respect for the power of rocks and gems, especially Amethyst!

Topaz

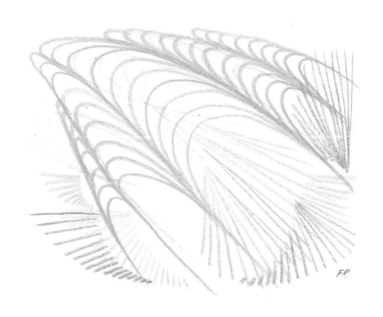

Blue lace agate

Blue sapphire

Since then I have drawn more Minerals, but have taken care to do them one at a time and on separate days. One thing I learned is that it is unwise to allow continuously high vibrations to flow through my body, as it causes imbalance, especially to my spine and head. I gave myself spaces of weeks of just getting on with my life, spending as much time as I could out of doors by the sea, in the sun and in nature, while accepting with joy all invitations from my wonderful friends.

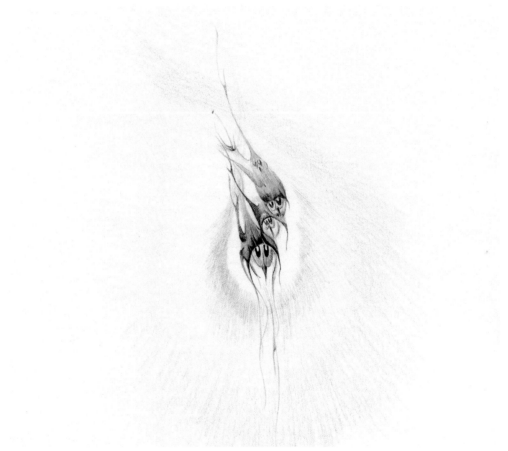

Insect Kingdom

Cut amethyst

The Seedpoint Drawings
and
a Visit to the Findhorn Foundation

From time to time I have received forms of drawing that I call my *Seedpoint* drawings. The *Seedpoint* drawings are composed of complex labyrinthine contours and colours, and seem, uniquely amongst my work, to be personal expressions regarding my inner state. I find these normally herald something new happening or germinating in my life. Through the *Seedpoint* drawings I could sense I was meant to be on the move.

✳✳✳

My Brighton landlord was being a little difficult, implying that I had only rented my two-room flat temporarily. Then suddenly one day he thumped on the door with his walking stick and announced that my rent was now doubled! When something seemingly awful is happening I usually find that I am not as alone as I feel, and it is usually part of a wider plan that will have a progressive outcome. Though it seemed a near disaster at the time, looking back I realise that I was resisting change and needed to learn to trust the process.

Knowing little or nothing about such matters of life, I was unaware that I was, in actual fact, clearing the impediments, tying up the loose ends, of relationships, home, mortgage commitments and so on. Unbeknown to me, my landlord's knock on the door was all in preparation for a very important life change. I started hunting for a place. Looking at many tiny flats and rooms I nearly took a small flat even closer to my work, but somehow I could not get it co-ordinated.

Then James, a close friend, who had been around at the time I first started the drawings suddenly, returned from Australia. Very interested and supportive, his presence brought a fresh breath of joy and enthusiasm. He almost immediately asked me to marry him. This was like spring in the depths of winter, and I

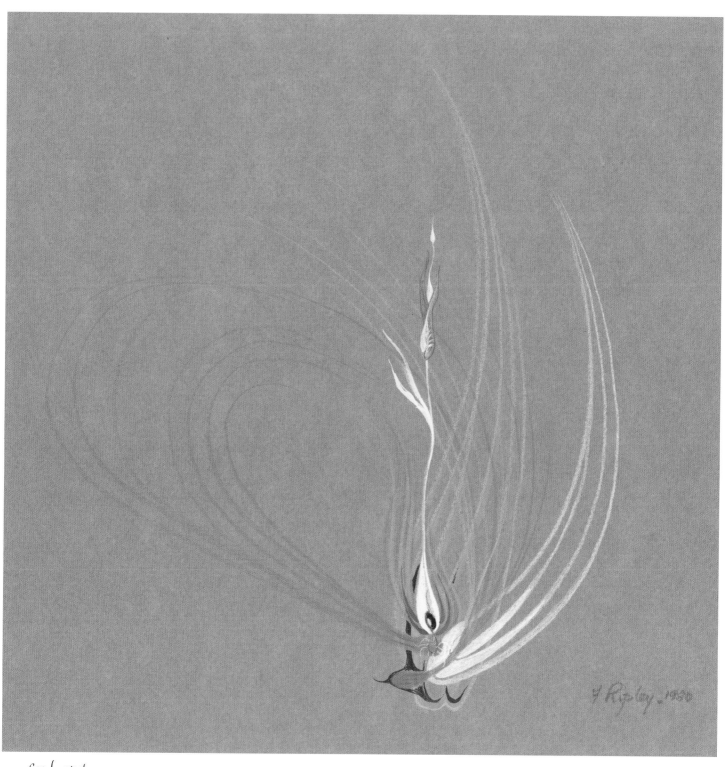

Seedpoint

accepted. We had a lot of fun, but very soon it became clear we had changed and did not really know each other. We had in fact fallen into the classic error of getting engaged for most of the wrong reasons.

After a few weeks I knew that James and I were working on two totally different life paths that were not going to meet. It was clear that somehow my life was not quite my own, as I had made a deep commitment to working for the Nature Kingdom and this way was now unfolding. Although I didn't know the direction, inwardly I instinctively knew that I had to set us both free again. This was a very strong conviction. In telling James of my reluctant decision I felt myself grow in stature. He said he saw the change in me even as I spoke. It was a strange and powerful experience for us both. After a long hug he said he did not feel that he could be just a friend. This was sad but understandable, and he later returned to Australia.

✳✳✳

For the time being I stayed put in my newly expensive flat, in spite of the inflated rent. But the Seedpoint drawings continued coming through, and there was a strong sense of change in the air. One day, while laying plans and contacting friends, I felt like drawing and seemed to have a very different energy around me. A star formation with a centre of light appeared in delicate, beautiful colours .

> *The centre of the star formation was gradually filled*
> *With a little sleepy-looking, childlike face*

Unlike any other face I had drawn. *An infant? Some newly arrived being?* I felt it was to be given to Anne. Carefully mounting it and wrapping it I included a little card with the inscription, *"Diana?"* The following day I gave it to her. When some weeks later I saw her again she said, "By the way, you knew before we did. I am pregnant again."

> *When Diana was born she looked exactly like the drawing.*

Now this posed an interesting question. There are many theories of when the

At conception

Soul enters the body. This experience showed us that Diana was around actually at conception. I knew nothing of the parents' intimate private lives and was in no way seeking information about their child. It came completely unexpectedly. To me it means that the Soul enters the body at conception and is a part of the growing embryo body. I have another similar infant drawing done some months later – this time in a drop of light rather than a star. Unfortunately I did not try to check it out when it was drawn, and I have not been able to trace the subject.

Around this time things were changing at the Farm and this was to prove of significance as to where my next step would take me. The group was not at this point so close; some members were turning their attention to other groups or activities. Anne was gravitating towards *Krishnamurti* who had his Centre very near by. I was interested but did not feel drawn to follow his path. Meanwhile I continued to receive the *Seedpoint* drawings.

I decided it was time to take a break and a trip north to Scotland again, spend time with family and friends and visit my beloved mountains. When I wrote to Anne that I was going on holiday to Scotland, she phoned back at once to say that, in the same post as my letter, she had received an envelope of information about a community in Scotland called the Findhorn Foundation.

As the correspondence had come together, she wondered whether there could be some significance. Would I go and visit the Foundation for our group while I was up? It also happened that the Foundation was putting on a whole-day presentation in London just before I was leaving, which our entire group decided to attend.

❋❋❋

The day proved magical. These happy, outgoing people had been packed into buses close to Inverness some 650 miles north. They had travelled overnight to London before launching straightaway into an amazingly full, joy-filled programme of song, dance and audio-visuals for our pleasure. There was something very different about them all; such love flowing in everything they did. Among other things, they showed a video about R. Ogilvie Crombie,

"Roc", who was in close and profound contact with all realms of the Nature Kingdom.

The founding members of the Findhorn Foundation, Eileen and Peter Caddy along with Dorothy Maclean, were at this time living in caravans in Findhorn. Dorothy had begun to communicate with the unseen worlds of the Devas in order to receive their guidance, which was to prove vital both for their physical and spiritual well-being. Roc was instrumental in extending the knowledge of these Worlds, and broadening the range of Beings contacted. These communications and relationships were the bedrock upon which the Findhorn Foundation was subsequently built.

There are many books on this subject so I will not expand on it here, except to say that as the video showed Roc telling of his experiences with the Nature Kingdom I became transfixed. As he described his contacts in such a real and calm way, I felt as if at last I had encountered an old, old friend. He actually spoke quite naturally and rationally about the extraordinary phenomena that I myself had been experiencing – and I had been *drawing* them just as he saw them. Here was a man I knew I had to meet. But I was told, "No, he does not live in the Community – a very private person, he lives somewhere in Edinburgh."

> *But still I knew clearly that I had to meet Roc.*

So, at the commencement of my holiday in September of 1972, I phoned to ask if I could have one night in the Foundation on return from my travels further north. *Yes, they had a bed.*

Driving down I arrived at a vibrant, lovely garden, finding myself among some 350 people, mainly American, but with many other nationalities as well. My bed was to be a minute bunk in a caravan full of Yugoslavs. Conversation was friendly but limited, and mostly in hasty sketches. Luckily, however, my guide for the day was English. All was fascinating – studios for weaving, pottery, candle-making, screen-printing and graphic design; a garden, sanctuary, Community Centre, and lots and lots of caravans. It was another world. The intense interaction and activity left me quite overwhelmed. I loved it all and it felt like home but at the same time I thought I could not live there.

When I asked if there was any possibility of meeting Roc, my guide produced an audio-tape of him talking about his experiences with the Nature Kingdom. We listened together, basking in the sun on a grassy bank.

> *This was a man with an amazing and rare connection*
> *With the Devic and Nature Spirit Realms.*

Roc saw them, and *conversed* with them. Even more I knew I must find him. However, my time had run out. I could not visit Roc in Edinburgh, as I had to return to Brighton for work the following day.

The following morning, one of the Foundation gardeners asked me if he could travel with me to Brighton as he wanted to visit his father. I was putting the car on the train and told him I had no money for a second ticket as I had already overdrawn to come up to Findhorn. He went silent a moment, then said, "I think it is going to be all right, I would like to come." And he turned on his heel and disappeared.

I was about to learn a profound lesson in living the Findhorn Foundation way of life, living by faith with no thought for where the next penny might come from, or if it was really needed.

My fellow-traveller shortly returned with the cost of the ticket in his hand. A friend had just received some unneeded money, so gave it to him. As I had a sleeper booked, I asked, "Will you sit up in the seating compartment, or have you enough for the extra cost of the sleeper?"

Again a pause, "I'll have a sleeper, please."

I booked him in as my passenger and got the last sleeper in the men's compartment. He came an hour later with the right sum, saying, "I have money for petrol and I will bring sandwiches for us both."

In those days I was an insecure, nervous and shy person. This was a new

Star of Hope

experience. I did not know this man at all, but it felt fine. We had a fascinating journey and we talked a lot about Roc and the Nature Spirits. We consumed a box full of delicious vegetarian sandwiches for dinner and breakfast, drove on from London to Brighton, and I delivered him to his father's home. He had money left over and absolutely insisted that it had been given to him for the journey and made me take it, leaving himself again with no money at all. Arriving home and opening my case I found someone had slipped an envelope in containing exactly what I had paid to go up and stay my twenty-four hours at the Findhorn Foundation.

I made up my mind there and then that Findhorn
Was where I would spend my next year's summer holiday!

I had always said firmly I would not go back to Scotland, but this was something totally different. Something had changed in me with this journey and brief visit to Findhorn. My travel companion had taught me a clear lesson in faith and manifestation, and demonstrated that I could do the same. The following year I booked for two weeks in July, and then discovered that Roc would be visiting there at the same time.

My Second Stay at Findhorn

In those days at the Foundation there were no workshops or any set programmes for visitors. You just had to be willing to do whatever was needed in any area. Everyone took a turn at cleaning. . .

> *Cleaning the toilets to perfection with love*
> *Being the prized experience!*

Any resentment and you found you would be left with the job! I worked at cleaning, cooking and also in the candle-making studio. Your learning was all day, in any place you were working, – eating meals, listening to tapes together, and of course attending Sanctuary twice a day. We worked at whatever was needed from 8:30am to 5:30pm, then were asked to change clothes and appear for dinner at 6:30pm. Usually there was some form of lecture, film or activity in the evening which we were all expected to attend. This was the regime seven days a week!

I found it overwhelming on the one hand, yet very special on the other. Drawings continued to come, although my sensitivity was without doubt being pressurised by the proximity of so many people. I achieved my ambition of meeting Roc briefly at this time, in spite of his being constantly in demand by everyone. As I had expected we instantly developed a close *rapport* which was later to grow into a deep and supportive friendship.

One day I was told that the right place to be drawing was in what was called the Middle Studio. This was one of the craft studios in the *Pineridge* area, some distance from the mobile home where I was staying. The building had very tall foxgloves growing in its garden, frequently visited by huge and lovely bumblebees.

I thought I would try tuning into a foxglove plant but as I did not feel free to break the stem, I sat down nearby and asked if I could draw something related to the plant.

Walking some four hundred yards over to the Studio, and finding just one other person quietly drawing, I settled myself close to an open window. My drawing was simple, like a vibrational pattern, and it was complete in about fifteen minutes, but what took place afterwards was fascinating. As I sat in the silence studying the drawing's simplicity, a large bumblebee flew in at the window straight to the drawing; then slowly buzzed its way spirally from the page up about four feet, facing inwards as it slowly hovered. After repeating the flight from bottom to top the bee zoomed back out of the open window. My drawing companion asked what had happened. Explaining the unusual journey the bee had taken around the drawing, she calmly replied, "It was probably looking for the flowers."

This sounded a bit far-fetched to me, so later I asked Roc. "Oh, *yes,*" he said. "The drawing is the vibrational pattern or field of the plant, and carries that vibration. The bee would in fact have been looking for the flowers because it is the vibrational field that they pick up and home in on to get the nectar."

Peter Caddy believed that you can ask plants to grow bigger, and his demonstration with flowers was with a foxglove in his own garden. He claimed it grew to eight feet. I tried the same in our garden by saying, "Please grow tall", as I passed the plant every day. It went up to seven-and-a-half feet. In the wild they grow about four feet tall.

> *If you would like to try it, choose a patch of several plants*
> *and ask one of them specifically to grow tall.*
> *That should give you a definitive demonstration.*
> *Or, if you have two clear patches,*
> *have one patch "normal" and the other tall.*
> *Just send the plant your love and ask it to grow tall,*
> *With the assistance of the Foxglove Deva, The Nature Beings*
> *Are very happy to give any co-operation we ask of them.*

On this my second visit to Findhorn I was now staying in the *Universal Foundation* bungalow. One day I had a rare couple of hours to do as I liked, so I went to the shop and bought a few things. On my way back

> *I caught my shy, reserved self*
> *Sort of skipping and dancing my way along.*

I could feel something round my legs tugging my slacks like a puppy trying to get my attention. I began to giggle uncontrollably. Whatever was happening to me? I tried to compose myself but back it came, persistent and friendly all the way to my bungalow. No one was there and I felt to miss lunch and *draw*.

The whole drawing proceeded in dots – lots of pencil and then colour; a ball-shaped body, a smaller ball for the head, long flowing rabbity ears. It was like drawing grains of sand held together with seawater. Dancing feet, like boots, and raised little arms with "hands", and eyes like a fish.

> *I was laughing away all the time*
> *With a feeling of fun and friendliness.*

It told me it was a *Sand Goblin (see next page)*. Thinking the drawing complete after an hour and having to return to my work in the candle-making studio, as I wrapped candles in cellophane I could feel this little Being trying to get my attention again. I reluctantly persuaded it to let me work until 5:30pm when I would be free. As I went home to my bungalow it was again tugging at my clothes. I knew I had to draw more. What could it be? When I sat with the pad and crayons I found it wanted the addition of an arc of sand between its hands. It had brought its own sand! Then it vanished.

A couple of days later I was with a group listening to an audio-tape about connecting with *devas*, by Dorothy Maclean. Intent and silent, we all listened. We were on the floor with hands round our knees. Suddenly I got a considerable prod in my ribs that made me jump and yelp. I could feel some annoyance at my unseemly behaviour. I was so embarrassed,

> *But how do you explain that*
> *you have just had a dig in the ribs from a* Sand Goblin?

I was unduly sharp with it in my thoughts and the Goblin vanished. It did not contact me again for about two months. I was so sad because I felt sure I had hurt its feelings. Sharing my experience with Roc, he told me that Nature Spirits don't have such feelings, and that it would return. And it did, about eight weeks later, still as joyful as ever. Roc left for home before I had a chance to talk with him at any length except to ask if perhaps I could visit him in Edinburgh on my way back south, and he very kindly invited me to lunch at his home.

Before I left the Foundation I was asked to talk with Peter Caddy, who at that time was responsible for saying who might come to live in the Community. Now I had not yet thought to live at Findhorn, but I found I was asking, "If one wanted to come, what is the procedure?"

Peter explained to me that British citizens were encouraged to buy their home – a caravan usually, as the site was in fact a caravan park. *"Above all, you would come to serve in whatever way was needed, pay a weekly contribution for your keep and provide for your own needs."* And Peter added, *"If you can manifest the means to come, you will know it is right to come."*

I put the idea to the back of my mind. I would have to give up my job. There was no such thing as paid work in the Foundation then, and I only had a very small sum in savings. Although my stay had been rich in experience, it was also hugely challenging. Most of the Community members at that time were American. To the sensitive and very retiring Scot in me, their outgoing and youthful energy was completely overpowering. *I was known for bursting into tears at the slightest provocation.*

I set off south with little thought of returning, heading first for Edinburgh to accept Roc's luncheon invitation. We had a simple and delicious lunch together and afterwards he asked to see my drawings. He was keenly interested, totally accepting, and understood precisely the process by which they had come. He seemed quietly excited at what I had drawn, particularly the latest one drawn at Findhorn, the *Sand Goblin*, whom he greeted with obvious complete recognition. I was surprised at his excitement and asked why he felt that way when he was already able to see and communicate with Nature Spirits and Devas.

> *"Ah, but you see, many people tell me,*
> *'I see Nature Spirits too,'*
> *but I have no way of knowing if they really do,*
> *and what they are actually seeing.*

Sand Goblin

Ripley, 1972

Sand Goblin

However, what you are drawing here is exactly what I see,
especially the Sand Goblin."

I told Roc I had been strongly challenged on this drawing by several people at the Foundation because he had described *Sand Goblins* in his taped talk. "No," he said, "I deliberately did not fully describe them. I did say they had a body like a ball and ears like a rabbit, but not that they had very short arms and legs, hands like claws and no toes."

I had not realised that my drawing had these features. What *elation* to now learn that this wonderful man saw exactly what I was drawing! We both felt the presence of the *Sand Goblin* in and around us as we were talking. Then somehow we fell silent for quite some time – a powerful silence, like a conversation at a Higher Level. I always say it was the most beautiful "conversation" I have ever experienced – not an earthly word spoken for about half an hour.

It was as if the room was filled with Nature Spirits.

I travelled down south with a glow of joy and peace all the way. What a privilege to meet such a special human being, wise, unassuming, delightful, with a lovely sense of humour, and also a truly Cosmic Being.

I later discovered that Roc's contact with the great god *Pan*, described in *The Findhorn Garden* occurred in 1966, the same year I began to receive the drawings.

Going to Live at the Findhorn Foundation

The following year, in August 1973, a brief letter came from Peter Caddy offering me the opportunity to buy a caravan in the Foundation. As I mentioned earlier, I had only enquired! As soon as this letter was in my hand, however, I knew I was going to Findhorn. The very next day another letter arrived, this from my mother who had decided to give me some of the proceeds from selling her house, as she always saw it as my real home. Suddenly I had just been presented with the means to both buy the caravan *and* pay my way at Findhorn for a whole year!

So gladly did I give in my notice to leave my teaching job that all were convinced I was returning to Scotland having fallen in love. In a sense, I had.

One of the staff asked if we knew of anyone selling a refrigerator. "Yes," I said, "come this evening and see it." *Had I any other things to sell?* Everything except the bed belonged to me. Unhesitatingly buying it all, even the carpets, he collected the lot two days later, leaving me just a few essential belongings and my suitcases, ready packed. Saying good-bye to my friends in the south was the hardest part, but I knew more clearly than ever that I had made the right decision. On the appointed day I coaxed my little groaning car up to London, and onto the Motor-Rail bound for Scotland.

Again visiting Roc in Edinburgh en route, in blissful silence we took a wonderful walk in the Royal Botanic Garden together. It was like being accepted into his special circle of Nature Beings. I certainly looked forward to living closer to him. Driving the last 150 miles north and arriving at Findhorn on September 21st, a brilliant, sunny day, I found a spotlessly clean, sparkling caravan, flowers and a bed all made up, all prepared lovingly by a group of housecarers.

> *This was the start of a very different life, not at all what I expected,*
> *As happens to most people who come to live at the Findhorn Foundation.*

Peter Caddy had felt guided to offer me the caravan because of my drawings. The Foundation was famous for its close if controversial co-operation with the

Nature Kingdom at that time, and, working in the garden, Peter thought I would now be able to produce lots of drawings of Nature Spirits. So convinced was he, that somehow we couldn't communicate.

Unable to conjure up drawings to order I needed time, and above all space and tranquillity, to be available to any Nature Being who might want to be drawn. Busily employed as I was like everyone else, from 8:30am to 5:30pm, at the end of the working day I was in no condition to receive and channel drawings. I felt very guilty, while Peter kept telling me to draw! This caused me such distress that I would frequently burst into tears. *I was put to watering the gardens!*

Some twenty years later Peter told me that eventually he had been afraid to speak to me. The fear was mutual! My sensitivity was no doubt due to the unusual pressure into which I had been drawn. Peter always made it clear that in order to stay in the Foundation you had to be able and willing to engage in hard physical work. Seen as essential, and applied ruthlessly in those early days, Peter's *regime* resulted in the impressively rapid growth of the Findhorn Foundation Community.

In retrospect it is clear that Peter was applying the same principle to my psychic work as had worked for him on the physical level. Of course, it did not apply. On the contrary, it blocked the process. Happily for me Roc intervened, helping Peter to see that I really had to be given more space if he wanted me to draw.

At last I did start to receive a few rare drawings, the first of which was the *Compost Gnome*. I was working afternoons in the gardens. We were all close to nature in many ways and used to meet and talk of our inner work and experiences and exchange information. One afternoon, having had a lovely tea together, we went home earlier than usual. My home at that time was a trailer right at the far end of the caravan site, the part now known as Bag End.

> *As I walked back, I was conscious of a Being coming with me.*
> *Not a joyful, bouncy Elf, but rather more earthy in feeling.*
>
> *I found myself experiencing the most extraordinary sensation.*

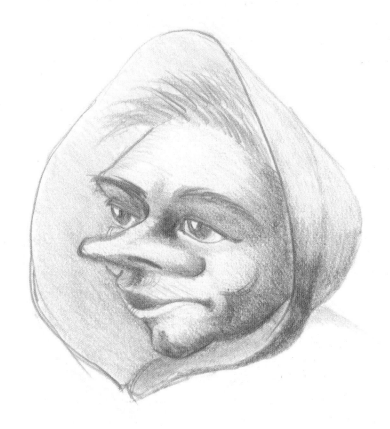

Francis Ripley

Compost Gnome 1973

Compost Gnome

I felt myself getting shorter and shorter, stocky,
Pacing steadily along with my feet getting bigger and bigger.

When I reached my caravan I sat down to draw. The brown and earthy *Compost Gnome* was drawn. I should explain that the Gnomes work with the soil and the earth, and they come in all shapes and sizes. This one felt to me to be about eighteen inches tall. I always hope that someday I may be given drawings of the *whole* Being, but up to now I only receive *heads* in detail, perhaps because it is hard for them to stay close for long enough for a whole "body" drawing to be completed.

The Sand Goblin *is the only complete body drawing,*
But then we have to be shown his completeness
To appreciate his unique "physiology".

On another occasion, soon after I had been talking with Roc, and still working in the garden very close to Nature, I once again felt the quick spirit of a Nature Being and I was shown to draw. It turned out to be a *Hazel Elf*, mischievous and joy-filled, and "he" obviously found it quite a challenge to stay steady to allow the drawing to happen.

I never did locate a hazel tree specifically, so *Hazel Elf* may have followed Roc from the Botanic Garden in Edinburgh.

The unique quality particular to faces is emphasised with the next drawing, *Duros*, which comes from the Findhorn Foundation's Cullerne Gardens, a conventional organic garden area that surrounds Cullerne House. As I sat leaning against a poplar trunk enjoying the peace of a lovely day, *Duros* came down out of the tree and I began to draw. Although I was aware of him I was not seeing him.

As I was happily drawing *Duros* and enjoying his company, the garden began to fill up with a group of lively, talkative guests from a workshop in the House. I tried an experiment. Telling *Duros* I would have to move to a quieter place, I invited him to come with me to my own tiny studio some 300 yards away down the road. He withdrew.

Hazel Elf.
Findhorn

F. Ripley 1978

Hazel Elf

Would he come with me? As I was settling at my place, *Duros* did join me again and the drawing was completed. I still didn't see him but I just knew he was there. Unfortunately I did not remember at the time to ask what *Duros's* particular "work" was, but now as I write I can feel him here and I am informed that his work is with the poplar tree.

❊❊❊

We all have the potential to see or feel the presence of unseen Beings.
But if you really truly ask to be able to see them
There is a responsibility in invoking them.
They long to work in co-operation with us humans,
But we need to be prepared to accept what shows itself to us.
It can be scary and disconcerting; some can appear really strange,
But also endearing or majestic in a humble way.

And so I slowly put my roots down at the Foundation, where I still live today.

Duros

Duros.
Cullerne.
1994
J. Ripley.

Devas of Place

There are Nature Spirits of plants and trees and there are also great Beings of the Landscape, which I call Devas of Place.

Iona

Traigh Bhan, a small cottage on the Island of Iona, off the West Coast of Scotland, is exposed to the Atlantic gales but has with it a simple and clear retreat energy. Findhorn Foundation Community members are encouraged to spend time there to recharge and reflect quietly, particularly at times of challenge or change in direction.

In the winter of 1977 or thereabouts, two of us who were working on the building of the Universal Hall at Findhorn needed a break. We were allowed to have *Traigh Bhan* to ourselves for a week.

At that time the crossing was at Minch in a small open boat shared with bales of straw, chickens and sheep, along with any other supplies for the Island, and of course Islanders and visitors. I am no sailor, and the stretch of water can be very turbulent with meeting currents. A storm was brewing as we crossed on the last sailing, dipping and rocking around alarmingly. We reached the Iona pier with our packs and food supply, and as there are no vehicles on the Island we had to fight our way against the wind to the cottage at the north end of the Island.

Traigh Bhan had single glazing, no insulation and a corrugated iron roof that leaked in various places. It was well nigh impossible to keep our feet if we went outside, so we were vitually marooned as the Force eight storm continued for five days. We lit the stove in the kitchen for cooking and hot water and there was a cheerful log fire in the living room. We spent our time reading, stoking fires, cooking and baking, listening to tapes and music, and just enjoying talking. On the fifth day we decided to tune in to the weather and see if some drawings might come. We both did a bit of scribbling. For me, these developed into a series of almost bird- or fish-like *Spirits of the Wind* whistling and howling as they progressed onto paper.

Dec 1997 Sina

F Kieley.

Spirits of the wind

Meanwhile, the house was being shaken and the rugs were flapping up on the floorboards. We greeted the *Spirits of the Wind* and asked them if they could possibly help us to get back onto the mainland, as we needed to return to work in Findhorn. Nothing changed for several hours, but by evening of the sixth day, the wind slackened, the sun appeared, and by the next morning the sea was comparatively calm and the ferry running again. It may well have been going to abate anyway, but we like to think our *Spirits of the Wind* had granted us our wish, at least in part.

A big bright rainbow was in the sky as we left.

Moray Firth

The Moray Firth is the stretch of seawater that lies on the East Coast of Scotland running in towards Inverness, passing Burghead, a small fishing town, and Findhorn Village, among many other small coastal communities.

On one occasion Roc had asked me to drive him over to Burghead, seven miles east along the shore from Findhorn. We wandered about in the Village and down by the harbour, soaking up the lovely, peaceful autumn day. The view of the Firth was sparkling and alive in some way. We stood quietly for some time, then

> *I became aware of the presence of a powerful and beautiful Being*
> *Unlike anything I had hitherto experienced.*

It was as if the Being was quite close behind us and was greeting us. Nothing was said, but as I reflect on that day, I feel it was a kind of introduction.

After we had returned to Findhorn, Roc told me it had been the *Deva of the Moray Firth* and that he would come to me to be drawn sometime later. But as always Roc gave me not a hint of what he would look like. It was several years

Deva of the Moray Firth

Moray Firth Deva
F. Ripley © 19

before the *Deva of Moray Firth* did come to me, but of course the Devas and other Nature Spirits do not live in time, and no doubt I was not in a sufficiently receptive state to welcome such a Being earlier. I had more or less forgotten Roc's prediction, and when the time came I had no idea what or whom I was about to draw.

Most of the drawing was done with the side of the pencil or crayon. I was drawing seaweed and water, as if the Deva was made of only things of the sea. The face began to build up, and moments before I actually drew the scales on his face, astonishingly I saw them on the paper. The features built up as I went along, very small areas at a time. The eyes were so clear and moist.

If you can, think of a Being over twenty-five feet tall.

This wonderful face is quite an overwhelming presence, a joyful, loving Being that welcomes anyone who accepts that he and his subjects of the Firth do exist. The Devas would not see themselves as Beings of high esteem in any kind of hierarchy. They are simply one aspect of Nature with their part to express.

Devas of the Landscape are static. They are Spirits of Place remaining in their particular area. Although the Sand Goblin is a part of this Realm, and has his specific work to do below on the beach and coastline, he can also move about. Roc had a Sand Goblin that visited him 150 miles south in his flat in Edinburgh.

> *When Roc expressed surprise, the* Sand Goblin *said,*
> *"Well you see you have not visited us for some time,*
> *So we thought we would visit you."*
> *Roc replied, "Don't you feel rather out of your element?"*
> *"No." said the* Sand Goblin. *"You see I have brought my own sand!"*

No doubt Roc's closeness of contact with the Nature Kingdom made it possible for the Nature Spirits to home in on him, though as I understand it, distance, like time, is something they do not comprehend. My experience of being with Roc out in Nature anywhere, was that we were always welcomed and surrounded with joyful Nature Spirits, hundreds of them.

Clarepoint Deva

One evening later in the year, I took Roc south of Forres to a beautiful nature area called *Randolph's Leap* – a narrow gorge through which the River Findhorn rushes, flanked by wonderful, majestic trees of many kinds.

It was full moon and it had been snowing. We were the first people to tread in the snow, blue and sparkling. A truly magical experience. The whole place was alive and teeming with Nature Spirits of all sizes. The very ground was covered with tiny Beings. I was almost afraid to take a step in case I did some damage! I could not, of course, because they are in another dimension, but it was very real to me.

The Deva of Moray Firth came to me some years after Roc had died, so, sadly, I was not able to show it to him for his comments. He will, I am sure, have seen it at another level. I can still feel Roc's presence at times like this.

Clarepoint

The name coming to me some time afterwards, the *Clarepoint Deva* was drawn in my small studio at Findhorn and started with the presence of a ball of light, which ultimately centred where the face is now drawn. The leafy foliage built up round the ball of light. This continued developing in such tantalising detail that I had to check myself from being curious. What, if anything, would finally appear in the ball of light space?

Then gradually the "pattern" of his eyebrows and nose was sketched in, and lastly the watchful penetrating eyes. Some people see it as a watchful and reproachful look, slightly feline. Like the *King of Beasts*, it is an example of a face that is both human and non-human. Disturbed while drawing this rather elusive Being, I haven't so far managed to reconnect with him.

As well as marking the end of a profoundly fruitful and active period, the *Clarepoint Deva* also heralded a new beginning and a major change of direction.

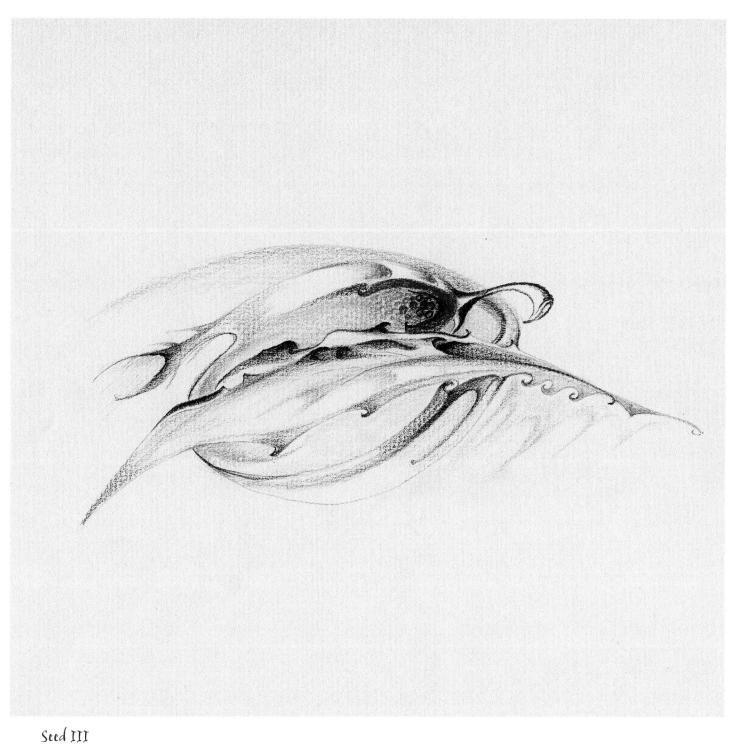

Seed III

A Visit to the South

Having married, a chapter in my life was naturally drawing to a close. After some time I moved with my husband George away from Findhorn to a tiny cottage on the moors south of Forres.

Closure on this part of my life did not happen all at once, however. At one point George had been asked to do some architectural work in the south of England and we decided to take the opportunity to combine a visit to some of our friends and relations. Then while George travelled to see his sister in Italy I went to Glastonbury, where Anne and David, my close friends from the Farm, now ran a Spiritual Centre.

Anne said they really would like a drawing of a Being she knew as the *"Keeper of the Oaks"*, as they had two magnificent oak trees growing in the garden. I had never attempted to request or even invite a specific Being to come to be drawn, but in this loving, understanding situation with my friends giving me their energy I accepted the challenge. They told me I could stay as long as it took to make the drawing. Anne knew never to tell me any details about Nature Beings except in confirmation after drawing.

Three days went by. I spent most of my time lying under the towering oaks or in the beautiful Sanctuary which nestled beneath its boughs, just soaking up a lovely natural energy. Withdrawing and disconnecting myself from the group, I grew distant and detached from the material sphere of the house and garden, and more and more aligned with the Nature Kingdom.

It was not until the fourth day that I began to feel I was actually to draw. I took my crayons and both large and small pads of paper to the Sanctuary. Feeling a friendly and inquisitive Being at my side I began to draw on my small pad. How these drawings are drawn is not my decision and this one came clearly and beautifully, in every detail.

> *A bright, happy little face emerged*
> *With oak leaves covering his head like a hat,*
> *And in a golden column of light.*

He was very intent and inquisitive and delightful. But somehow I did not think

oak 2N.

© F. Ripley 1982.

Oak Elf

this was the *Keeper of the Oaks*, though this *Oak Elf* was certainly from the tree. Then I thought that perhaps he had come to see what I was doing – to check me out, so to speak. So I asked him to return, and then said in my mind (for you do not have to speak out loud), "Now that you see what I do, people in the house would very much like to have the privilege of a drawing of the '*Keeper of the Oaks.*' Could you please ask if he would give us this pleasure?" I then waited some twenty minutes after which I began to feel decidedly strange.

> *It was as if I had become part of the tree, inside the trunk*
> *With the sap flowing all round me up the trunk,*
> *All green and brown and vibrant.*

A feeling of infinite wisdom and timelessness prevailed, linked with the centre of the earth and reaching up to the sun and the stars. I had disappeared.

Then I started to draw. The large pad was barely big enough. The softest pencil was taken and the drawing was done with the side of the lead. Charcoal might have been more suitable had I had it to hand. I had never drawn in such a dynamic way. From bottom to top it rushed. Every stroke went from bottom to top quite quickly. Every so often it would add a little more to the face appearing in the centre, but always somehow missing the eyes.

The sockets stayed clear despite the speed of the drawing. When all else was complete, the wonderful eyes were drawn in. His eyes somehow came alive as they do in the drawing lying beside me as I write. I can feel this magnificent Presence approving of my telling you about our encounter. His name is *Axel – The Keeper of the Oaks*. With the drawings complete I went into the house to show what had come. Anne recognised *Axel* at once and was delighted with both drawings. They gave me a lovely meal as I had missed my lunch, and we talked on into the evening.

Several years later, when living again at Findhorn, I suddenly switched on the television set and recognised Anne was being interviewed. It was a programme showing disputes between neighbours. Although having plenty of land elsewhere to site his new house, Anne's neighbour was fighting for permission

Keeper of the Oaks

to build right on the roots of her precious oak. In that moment I realised I had switched on the TV at an unusual time for us. This was *Axel's* tree, and I had been made aware of our friends' challenge!

At this point Axel appeared to me in Findhorn, 675 miles away, to tell me that no matter the lengths to which the neighbour went, he would not succeed in damaging the roots of this tree. I immediately telephoned Anne to give her the news. We had not been in touch for several years and she was delighted. What could have happened here was that Anne may have been too upset with what was happening to be calm enough for *Axel* to have reassured her. So I had been linked in to convey the message. Needless to say, the tree was not damaged, and I was delighted to be able to help Axel and Anne again.

This communication came to me out of the blue. I am not a special person. Surely communications like this can and would happen for all of us, if only we accepted them as possible and true. How much more help and guidance might be available to us if only we made space in our lives to be still, listen and reflect.

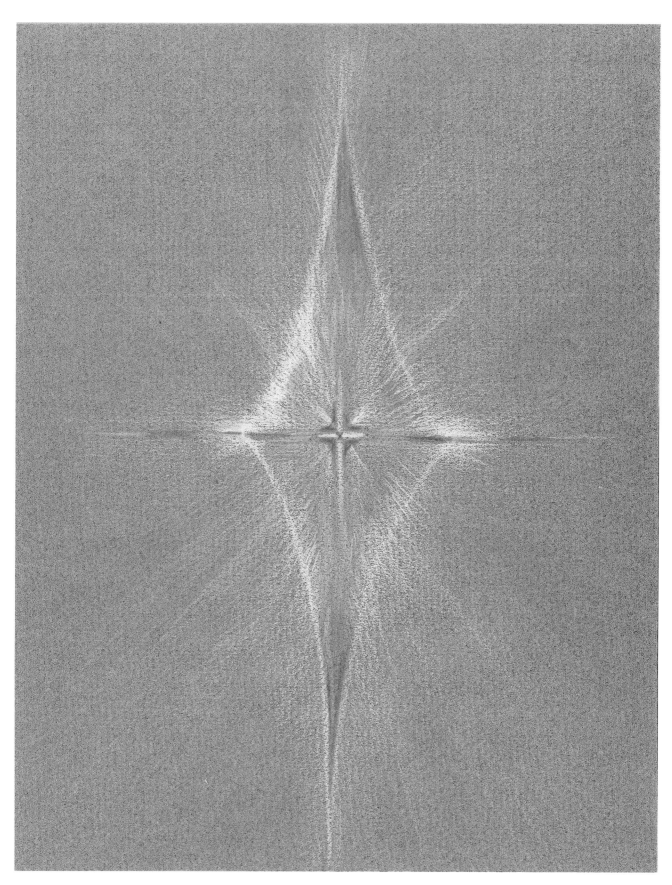

Star of Peace

Epilogue

In 1992 I received what has so far proved to be the final drawing; it is as yet unnamed. People frequently ask, "Why no more drawings?" My answer is twofold.

Firstly, it is important to remember that it is the Nature Spirits and Devas who choose to make connections. Our task, in order to receive a Transmission, is to be in a space of contentment, calm and freedom from stress. One needs to create a "field" of open-mindedness, a state which is focused but not limiting in any way whatsoever – that is to say, a feeling of readiness and availability, devoid of expectations. It might be described as a non-directional space, tinged with a sense of welcome and hope. A "supportive presence", if you like, which enables one to tune into the vibrational flow of the Being. Devas and Nature Beings possess infinite wisdom and will continue the work as and when the circumstances are right.

Secondly, it is not uncommon for mediums and persons with a strong psychic awareness to suffer from heart problems, as in fact did Roc. I am no exception. Nature Beings and Devas have their own magnetic force, which, as I have stated, affected my heart rate, either quickening its pace or slowing it down. It is clear that this kind of work demands considerable physical robustness and it is possible they know that I, at present, do not possess this.

Another question I am asked is, "Why? What is the purpose of these perceptions and drawings?" There are various responses to this and one can only surmise. Some have explained at length the – at this time – crucial teaching these Unseen Messengers have to give, and I will simply echo that they are urging and encouraging us to live carefully, mindfully, and in harmony with Nature. There exists therefore a need and a desire on the part of the Nature Beings and Devas for us humans to become aware of their existence, and to acknowledge them as a reality.

Also they may wish to share and communicate the feeling of profound joy and love present in the universe. They choose consequently to become visible sometimes and show themselves to those who can record them with pencil and paper, or in whatever medium, and thus become known more widely.

The Crown of Progression

Furthermore, there is a natural thirst for people to wonder what these Ethereal Beings look like and where they live. I was given the privilege of presenting their appearance in drawings. Because we dwell in the material realm, people often need proof and verification before they can believe in the idea of metaphysical planes. And in fact I myself always felt better when my perceptions were verified and confirmed by others, as was the case, for instance, initially with *Lennie* and, much later, the *Sand Goblin*, and on many other occasions by Roc.

It occurs to me, too, that the drawings may be used as a focus for meditation or endeavour. For instance, if one wished either to compose a piece of music, to gain a deeper soul understanding of an existing composition, or indeed to develop an insight into the composer's intention, one might use the *Master of Sound*. Similarly, if one wanted to form a profound connection with an aspect of the seashore, one might achieve this with the aid of the *Sand Goblin*. An ailing hazel tree might communicate its needs and wishes through the *Hazel Elf* and valuable guidance for restoring the precious balance of Nature might be received.

I would add that it feels important for us to develop our own insights and intuitions with regard to how we employ the images of Nature Spirits and Devas. It is worth considering that they may, at this moment, be handing over the responsibility to us to divine the next steps towards gleaning Universal Wisdom and truth through fusion with the unseen worlds. Everyone has the potential to nurture this side of their consciousness if they are inclined to open up to the presence of these unseen Beings.

Although the process for me is for the time being "on hold", I am fortunate enough to be able to say that I am living very happily and contentedly, and I have a sense that I am open and receptive while awaiting the advent of the next phase. Who knows, the writing of this book, chronicling my past experiences, may be the very thing that will herald whatever is to follow.

For further information about the Findhorn Foundation and the Findhorn Community,
please contact:

Findhorn Foundation

The Visitors Centre
The Park, Findhorn IV36 3TZ, Scotland, UK
tel 01309 690311
enquiries@findhorn.org
www.findhorn.org

For a complete Findhorn Press catalogue, please contact:

Findhorn Press

305a The Park, Findhorn
Forres IV36 3TE
Scotland, UK
tel 01309 690582
fax 01309 690036
info@findhornpress.com
www.findhornpress.com